To Rick
Walk with the Lord!
Joshua 1:9
Tim Gallop

THE GOLFER'S BOOK OF PROVERBS

31 Things God taught me about life while playing golf

A Daily Devotional Book for Those Who Love Golf

BY TIM GALLOPS

CROSS

BOOKS

CrossBooks™
1663 Liberty Drive
Bloomington, IN 47403
www.crossbooks.com
Phone: 1-866-879-0502

First published by CrossBooks 11/18/2009

ISBN: 978-1-6150-7061-9 (sc)

Library of Congress Control Number: 2009941806

*Printed in the United States of America
Bloomington, Indiana*

This book is printed on acid-free paper.

TO ROBIN, MY WIFE AND MY PLAYING PARTNER
IN LIFE

TABLE OF CONTENTS

FORWARD

If you are buying this book, then in all probability, you have the same two passions in life as I do: the game of golf and my Christian walk. For whatever reason, God has chosen this game to demonstrate to me many of His truths and life lessons. He has used these examples to help me become a better person and to help me live a more consistent Christian life.

Similar to becoming a Christian, when you decide to become a golfer, there is a cost involved. You have to buy clubs, balls, shoes, gloves, proper clothes and perhaps even join a golf or country club. With all that said, taking up this great game is not cheap and neither is living the Christian life. When you take up your cross and follow Him, make no mistake, there is a cost involved from the world's viewpoint. During my life, following Christ has cost me friends, promotions, positions and money. Any regrets have been short lived. So, though vastly different, both passions involve serious costs.

There is an anonymous poem that describes this great game that I love so much. It is simply called "*The Greatest Game*". It could also describe our life as a Christian. Here it is.

> Golf is deceptively simple and endlessly complicated.
> A child can play it well, and a grown man can never master it.

Any single round of it is full of unexpected triumphs and seemingly perfect shots that end in disaster.

It is almost a science, yet it is a puzzle without an answer. It is gratifying and tantalizing, precise and unpredictable.

It requires complete concentration and total relaxation. It satisfies the soul and frustrates the intellect.

It is at the same time rewarding and maddening -- and it is, without a doubt, the greatest game mankind has ever invented.

I have often thought that if Jesus had played sports, one he would have enjoyed would have been the game of golf. It is perhaps the one sport that demonstrates our Christian walk....... or not. As no other game can do, golf will bring out what is in your heart. I hope you enjoy reading this Golfer's Book of Proverbs. I hope God will bless you as He has me. Enjoy the round. Enjoy your walk with God.

Day 1

GETTING STARTED

Usually, I will put the Bible verses at the end of each of the daily devotions. Today will be the exception. I believe there is one verse in the Bible that sums up the essence of the passionate golfer. It is located in the Book of Romans. It's a short verse that is actually in the middle of one of Paul's long sentences for which he is known. It is Romans 12:12, "*rejoicing in hope, persevering in tribulation, devoted to prayer*".

Let me break it down for you. The first phrase is "rejoicing in hope". To me this means that, even though you play the same course over and over, and even though the holes are in relatively the same place, each round of golf is brand new. Each round is a new game. Each course is a new challenge. Similarly, every day is new and we get to decide what we will do with it. We can dwell on what happened yesterday or rejoice in what God has in store for us. When I step up on the first tee box, I have hope that this time the practice will pay off, that I will maintain the proper swing plane and putt the ball in the hole.

The second phrase is "persevering in tribulation". Sometimes even well executed shots go awry. You hit a good shot; it takes a bad bounce and lands in a hazard. Golf and life are unpredictable. Sometimes your

1

weaknesses get the best of you. You fall into old habits, both on and off the golf course. You have to learn to play through those tough results when the golf course treats you badly and when life deals you a low blow. To overcome these situations, you must become devoted. To get better at golf, you must dedicate yourself to the game. To get better at life, you must acknowledge your weaknesses and pray daily about them. Generally, we tend to practice what we are already good at. We should celebrate our strengths and also practice and work on our weaknesses.

Finally, this verse ends with "devoted to prayer". In golf, you can buy all sorts of swing aids to improve your game. I have them, so do you. But you know what; you still have to play the game with balls and clubs that are approved. In the same way, commentaries are good and books like this one will help. However, they are no substitute for studying your own Bible and spending time in prayer. Decide today to have a daily quiet time with God.

Day 2

PRACTICE ROUTINES

I am always amazed at how most amateur golfers approach the game compared to the pros. Many will arrive early to practice before a friendly round. If they have thirty minutes to warm up, twenty five of those minutes will be spent on the practice tee and most of that time will be used with a driver in their hands. Very little, if any, time will be spent on the practice green getting a feel for the speed and grain of the putting surface. Statistics show that over 60% of shots are from less than 100 yards. So, your time would be better used chipping and putting.

Many of us approach our Christian walk in the same way. We are very proficient at resisting the sins described in the Ten Commandments; you know stealing, murder, adultery and the like. However, we are not very good at keeping pure with regard to what is valued by us as lesser sins. In fact, we often over look or excuse them. Sins such as overeating, gossip, cheating on our taxes or laziness are still sins. What must be remembered here is that while we humans value sin, God does not. He sees them all as falling short of the mark.

In the game of golf a missed three foot putt costs the same as a 270 yard drive on your scorecard. In the game of life, God tells us to resist all sin. You see, it's these little sins in our life, (you have yours and I have mine), that keep us from being really close to God. These sins can also hurt or sometimes ruin our witness. Just as that missed chip or putt keeps us from breaking 80, little sins can undermine our Christian walk and reputation. Learn to use your practice time wisely and keep your whole game sharp, in life and on the golf course.

SWING THOUGHT FOR THE DAY

For all have sinned, and fall short of the glory of God; being justified as a gift by
His grace through the redemption which is in Christ Jesus.
Romans 3: 23-24

Day 3

VISUALIZATION

There is one thing that I believe all great golfers do. They have the uncanny ability to visualize the shot they need to make at that moment, and usually under a great deal of pressure. They are able to visualize the club striking the ball, the flight of the golf ball, where it lands on the green, how it needs to release and then roll to the hole. They also see the ball going into the hole on every putt. This trait is no accident. It is worked on like every other aspect of the game. Over time, it builds confidence and lowers scores.

Great men of the Bible had this ability too. Moses visualized the Israelites going into the Promised Land. David saw the defeat of the giant, Goliath as he chose the stones for his sling. Nehemiah was able to see the rebuilding of the walls around Jerusalem. Peter had the vision of building a great church by going to the Jewish nation. Paul, too, had a similar vision, but he went to the rest of the world. What about you? What kind of visions do you have for your life? Have you sought a vision from God? Do you know where God is leading you and into what kind of service? The world says, "When I see it, I'll believe it". The man of God should say, "When I believe it, I'll see it".

You see, great golfers have that acquired ability to visualize a shot. They also have the faith that they, after long hours of practice, will execute the shot just the way they saw it in their minds. How about your faith? Do you see yourself being used by God? Take a minute today and seek a vision from God. Then, have the faith to carry it out. The next time you have a testy six footer to save par, remember the time you spent on the practice green. Stroke it confidently and watch it go in the hole.

SWING THOUGHT FOR THE DAY

Now faith is the substance of things hoped for, the evidence things not seen. **Hebrews 11:1**

Day 4

THE PERFECT ROUND

Most of us have a favorite professional golfer, either past or present or both. Without question, my favorite golfer was and always will be Ben Hogan. His accomplishments, work ethic and dedication to the sport are to be admired. His record speaks for itself. I remember on one occasion, Mr. Hogan had shot an unbelievably great round of golf on a very difficult course. Afterwards, during the press conference, he was asked if he had played the perfect round of golf. He immediately said no. He went on to say that the perfect round of golf consisted of making a birdie on every hole which would result in a score of 18 under par. As you can see, using that definition, the perfect round will never be played. It's impossible; no one will ever be that good.

What's this got to do with our Christian walk? Well, we are asked to live a sinless life. Can this be done? Certainly not. So far, only ONE has been able to accomplish this. Yet, throughout the New Testament, we are encouraged to struggle for this goal. Why even try if it's impossible? The reason is that with every effort, every time we persevere, every time we put others first, every time we love as He loves us, every time we are patient, we become a little more like Jesus and a little less like the world. That, to me, is enough. Too often, we compare ourselves with others and excuse our poor behavior by saying we are not as bad as this person or that person. Remember, the yardstick, the gold standard if you will, is Jesus. We must continue to strive for that type of excellence and perfection, both on and off the golf course. So, even though the perfect round of golf will never be played, people in ever increasing numbers continue to take up the game of golf. Similarly, we should never give up on our Christian journey. If we endure, it will be worth it all when we here the words, "Well done, good and faithful servant. Enter into my rest".

SWING THOUGHT FOR THE DAY

So then each one of us shall give account of himself to God. Therefore, let us not judge one another anymore: but rather determine this - not to put an obstacle or stumbling block in a brother's way. **Romans 14: 12-13**

◀━━━

Day 5

COMMITMENT

Golf is a sport that requires a certain amount of dedication and passion to become proficient. As I mentioned in the forward, it's an expensive game and, if you remember the anonymous writing, "it frustrates the intellect and satisfies the soul". To pursue this game you may have to give up several if not all of your remaining hobbies. It is for these reasons and many others that I believe God has chosen this game (for me at least) to demonstrate how this past time mirrors our Christian walk.

I have a friend who is a gifted athlete in many sports. He is very good at most of them. However, he plays golf about three times a year. On every occasion, golf humbles him. Golf is not a sport that allows you to just dabble, playing once in a while and scoring well. Our Christian walk is like this. Our God is a jealous God. He requires that we follow Him completely, leaving no room for other spiritual activities. God wants us to enter the struggle of the Christian life full time. I think "struggle" is the right word here because we will not be perfect. No one except Jesus ever has been. As mentioned earlier, no one has ever played the perfect round of golf, but we keep at it, learning from our mistakes and celebrating those few perfectly executed shots. Similarly, you can't show up to church on Thanksgiving, Christmas, Easter and Mother's

Day and be considered a strong Christian. Many times in the gospels, Jesus warned of those that gave God lip service, following him only when it was convenient. Jesus wants us to follow Him fully and completely. That is the price of a God-pleasing Christian walk.

Like golf, to be a Christian also means you are to be active. You can't just watch a tournament on television and call yourself a golfer. And you can't be a useful Christian and just watch every thing happen around you. The name Christian implies action. It takes practice, perseverance and patience to be called either a golfer or a Christian. Go on, get in the game.

SWING THOUGHT FOR THE DAY

No one can serve two masters: for either he will hate the one, and love the other; or he will hold to the one, and despise the other. Ye cannot serve God and mammon. **Matthew 6:24**

Day 6

PRESHOT ROUTINE

When golfers warm up prior to a match, they will practice routine shots as well as shots that they believe they will need during the round. Also, if you watch any particular pro golfer, before long you notice that he will do certain things over and over before every shot. This is called a preshot routine. Some golfers always take a practice swing. Some golfers line up a putt from behind the ball and at address they have a forward press of the putter. These routines let the body know that the mind is ready to execute the shot. Most golfers have them. I have mine, you have yours. And, for the most part they work.

Sharing our witness with others is sort of like preparing for a golf match. It is helpful to study a witnessing method and practice before actually going out and doing it. There are several well known, tried and true methods for sharing Jesus with others. Pick one and stick with it.

Now, whether you are on the golf course or the witness field, go through your preshot routine and execute the shot. Once you do, accept the results and move on. I have hit some really good shots in golf that have had miserable results. I have also witnessed effectively with very little or no results. Dwelling on a bad result in golf can sometimes ruin an otherwise good round. Likewise, becoming disappointed when rejection takes place may keep you from witnessing to the next person God sends your way. When you witness, trust God for the results. Remember they are not rejecting you, they are rejecting God. You don't save people, God through the Holy Spirit does. So, whether on the course or off, pick a routine and stick with it. The results will come.

SWING THOUGHT FOR THE DAY

Preach the word; be ready in season and out of season; reprove, rebuke, exhort, with great patience and instruction. For the time will come when they will not endure sound doctrine; but wanting to have their ears tickled, they will accumulate for themselves teachers in accordance to their own desires; And will turn away their ears from the truth, and will turn aside to myths. But you, be sober in all things, endure hardship, do the work of an evangelist, fulfill your ministry. **II Timothy 4: 2-5**

Day 7

LOVE YOUR ENEMIES

Many years ago, I had the opportunity to play the TPC course at Sawgrass, just outside of Jacksonville, Florida. Because of this, the Players Championship is one of my favorite tournaments to watch. In 2004, Adam Scott won the tournament. This is a major accomplishment for any pro golfer. What interested me about this was a comment he made during the interview after he had won. He gave most of the credit for his win to a fellow competitor, Greg Norman. When questioned about this, he went on to say that earlier that week, he was having trouble on the practice tee with a particular shot. Mr. Norman happened to be practicing at the same time and noticed something in his swing. He could tell that Adam was struggling and offered to help. The help was accepted and the advice he gave to the young golfer helped him to be victorious.

How cool is it that golf is a game where you actually help your competitor or enemy, so to speak. I believe that God expects us to do the same. We all have our adversaries on and off the course. There have been times when a fellow competitor was about to do something that would cost him a stroke such as forgetting to replace his ball mark properly on the green. I don't like winning in this manner so I remind them. I fix spike marks and ball marks on the green. Honorable golfers will also help their competitor hunt for a lost ball so he does not incur a stroke and distance penalty. Off the course, we all have co workers that we just don't get along with. I believe the Bible encourages us to help them anyway and win them over. We are commanded to love unconditionally, as Jesus did. Just as the game of golf separates itself from other sports by acts such as these, so too should we separate ourselves from the world by helping those who work against or antagonize us. Developing this habit will result in a skill that will almost always make you part of the solution to every problem. Love is a trait that never goes out of style.

Swing Thought for the Day

Be devoted to one another with brotherly love; give preference to one another in honor.
But if your enemy is hungry, feed him; and if he is thirsty, give him a drink: for in so
doing you will heap coals of fire on his head. Do no be overcome of evil,
but overcome evil with good. **Romans 12: 10, 20-21**

Day 8

CONTROL ISSUES

Most of us have a home course that we play more than any other. In fact, we usually play the same one over and over. The interesting thing about this is that while it's the same course, we encounter an endless variety of situations, seemingly on every round of golf we play. Many of these events are totally out of our control, which really irritates us. Sometimes it's a contrary wind, an unraked bunker, your ball coming to rest in a divot, a bad kick off a sprinkler head into a hazard or other events known as the "rub of the green". These things happen and you can not ignore them. You have to account for them and adjust your game accordingly. Ultimately, it comes down to relying on the confidence you gained from meaningful practice and trusting your swing. By using your experience, skill and a positive attitude, a good swing will result in acceptable results more often than not.

So too, in life, you will face a myriad of events over which you have no control. They will consume your energy and time and cause you to become ineffective at work, church and home. Jesus reminded us not to waste a lot of time worrying about these issues. Do you remember the questions He asked of the people of that day? He asked them who could extend their life by one day, or who could add inches to their height by worrying. None of them could and neither can you. Worrying about these things will simply weigh you down. Rather, spend your time on things that you can control such as your heart rate, your composure and emotions. Work on these and watch your game improve. Just as you trust your swing on the golf course, learn to trust in your Lord when you face these life situations.

SWING THOUGHT FOR THE DAY

And which of you by being anxious can add a single cubit to his life's span? If then you
cannot do even a very little thing, why are you anxious about other matters?
Consider the lilies, how they grow; they neither toil nor do they spin;
but I tell you, even Solomon in all his glory did not clothe himself like one of these. **Luke 12: 25-27**

Day 9

MOLDED FOR USE

Golf clubs and golf club technology have improved dramatically over the last fifteen or twenty years. Clubs are cast for forgiveness or forged for workability. Several new materials such as steel, graphite and titanium are now used in the production of golf clubs. There are also urethane and ceramic inserts. You can buy blades or cavity backs depending on your level of competence. And the list goes on and on. No matter which clubs you choose, they all share some things in common. Most of them are made with high temperatures and extreme pressures. By going through these processes, a hunk of iron becomes a useable and sometimes expensive product. (They have great value in the hands of an expert.) Another thing these products share is that they all made the transition from raw material to product via the hands of a master craftsman. You see, the best ingredients in the world are of little use or value without the knowledge and expertise of the club maker.

Once we give our hearts to Jesus, God begins to mold us into useful vessels. As this happens, sometimes we too go through trials and rough times that temper us, thereby making us stronger and more ready to be used by our maker. So the next time you feel the heat and pressure of being in this world, remember that it is the trials and tribulations that make us tougher and stronger. Then, with the help of the master craftsman, the Lord Jesus, we are transformed into valuable and precious instruments of ministry for Him. Often times when we come through these times, we are then uniquely qualified to minister to others. Look for those opportunities.

SWING THOUGHT FOR THE DAY

And so, as those who have been chosen of God, holy and beloved, put on a heart of
compassion, kindness, humility, gentleness and patience; bearing with one
another, and forgiving each other, whoever has a complaint against
anyone; just as the Lord forgave you, so also should you. And beyond all these things put on love, which is the perfect bond of unity. And let the peace of Christ rule in your hearts, to which indeed you were called in one body; and be thankful.
Colossians 3: 12-15

Day 10

FORGIVENESS

Almost everyone warms up prior to a round in one way or another. For me, this routine includes stretching, putting, then chipping and putting once more. I swing two clubs to get loose and then I am ready to go. Then, hopefully, I hit my tee shot down the middle. Next, for whatever reason, I sometimes execute my second shot poorly and it ends up in the woods on the right or that pesky ditch on the left side of the fairway. What happens next is very important. I am usually left with two choices. I can dwell on the previous shot and let it consume me; or I can forget it and concentrate on the next shot. When I have been able to do the latter, I often go on to have a pretty good round. When I dwell on the mistakes, I usually press and things get worse. Successful players on the tour seem to have developed this ability to have a short memory where their errors are concerned. This is a key ingredient to success on and off the golf course.

I believe forgiveness works the same way. During our lifetime, all of us will need to give and receive forgiveness numerous times. If you have wronged someone, go to them and ask for forgiveness and learn to leave it there. If you have sinned against God, He is ready to forgive as well. Probably the hardest thing to do, however, is to learn to forgive ourselves. Though we often go to God and ask His forgiveness, (He gives it freely), we continue to beat ourselves up over the matter, often times, over and over. By doing this, we allow Satan to affect us in one of the few ways he can. If we are saved, he can no longer have our souls, but he is happy to ruin our witness and our effectiveness as a Christian. Learn to forgive yourself quickly and completely. It will make your life better on and off the golf course.

Swing Thought for the Day

If therefore you are presenting your offering at the altar, and there remember that your
brother has something against you, leave your offering there before the altar,
and go your way; first be reconciled to your brother, and then come
and present your offering. **Matthew 5: 23-24**

Day 11

LISTEN TO YOUR COACH

I took up the game of golf when I was in my late thirties. I was more or less self taught. The result of this was several bad habits which resulted in a poor golf swing and scores in the upper nineties. I had a friend in very much the same situation. However, our approach to getting better differed greatly. You see, he decided to go out and buy a game. He purchased all the latest equipment. It helped some, but not much. I decided to go to a teaching pro and take lessons. I figured that I needed advice from someone who knew what a good swing looks like and how to teach it to me. One of the techniques he used was to record my swing and then down load it on a computer. Next, he put my swing next to the swing of a tour pro. As you might guess, my swing was nowhere near as good as the pros. So why do this? Well by having a direct comparison, it is easier to see what you need to work on and improve. During the series of lessons I successfully stopped several poor habits and replaced them with good ones. This resulted in a fairly simple and repeatable swing. Well, after spending about half of what my friend did, I can now beat him at will.

In the same way, when we want to improve our Christian walk, we must also go to an expert in this area, Jesus. By making Jesus our example, studying God's word and regularly attending church, the Holy Spirit will begin to show you habits and activities that you should stop. Gradually, with a lot of effort and prayer, these will be replaced with sound practices that make us a little more like Him, thus improving your spiritual golf swing. It's important to remember that it is not enough to just break bad habits. If you don't fill those voids with good ones, you will be susceptible to return to the old ones. All of us need to be coached from time to time, both on and off the golf course. Even the greatest golfers in the world take golf lessons and so should Christians who wish to have great faith. That's how both groups maintain their high level of performance and effectiveness.

SWING THOUGHT FOR THE DAY

Be diligent to present yourself approved to God as a workman who does not need to be
ashamed, handling accurately the word of truth. But avoid worldly and empty
chatter, for it will lead to further ungodliness.
II Timothy 2: 15-16

Day 12

THE FUNDAMENTALS

Earlier, I mentioned that I went to a golf academy when I made the commitment to be a better golfer. After watching me hit a few balls, my instructor decided that I needed to work on some fundamentals. He told me to get better; there were three things I would have to master: my stance, my grip and ball position. Without doing these properly time after time, I would never realize my potential. First, I worked on my stance. My feet needed to be parallel to the target and shoulder length apart. I needed to bend from the hips and keep my back straight. Next, we worked on my grip. I should grip the club so I could see two, maybe two and a half knuckles. My right thumb should be on top of the grip. This would make the V's formed by my thumbs and index fingers point to my right shoulder. Finally, we checked my ball position. For most shots, I simply needed to keep the ball in the middle of my stance. Once I got these three things right, my game began to improve, just as my instructor said they would.

I believe that a good and satisfying relationship with God begins and is built upon fundamentals as well. After becoming a Christian, each of us starts down a path that hopefully will develop us into a mature Christian. This involves understanding, grasping and holding onto certain fundamentals of our faith. We may all chose different ones, however, they are very important absolutes that will anchor our faith and without which, we will never reach our potential for God. You see, we live in a world where, according to secular standards, very few things are absolutely right or wrong. This philosophy contends that most issues are situational and depends on the circumstances. I submit to you that this will lead to a mediocre life, and if you are a Christian, a life most miserable. My fundamentals include the Bible being God's word with no mistakes, Christ being virgin born and God's only son and the permanency of salvation. What are yours? If you don't know, find them and watch your game improve on the golf course. Find them in your spiritual life and watch you relationship with God become rock solid.

SWING THOUGHT FOR THE DAY

For this is contained in scripture: "Behold I lay in Zion a choice stone, a precious cornerstone. A stone of stumbling and a rock of offense"; for they stumble because they are disobedient to the word, and to his doom they were also appointed. But you are a chosen race, a royal priesthood, a holy nation, a people for God's own possession, that you may proclaim the excellencies of Him who has called you out of darkness into His marvelous light. **I Peter 2: 6a, 8-9**

Day 13

Improving from the Inside Out

Have you ever wondered how the golf ball came about? That would probably make for an interesting study, but sadly, it is out of the scope of this devotion book. What I do want to talk about is the improvements that have been made to the golf ball, especially the last several years. During this time, however, the cover of the golf ball has pretty much stayed the same. Basically, there are two materials that almost all golf ball covers are made of, isomers and ionomers. These are two types of plastic. So if this is true, how has the golf ball been improved so much? Well, most of the improvements have been made on the inside. Today, you can buy golf balls with a two piece center, a three piece center, balls with a tungsten core, balls with a titanium core and the list goes on. Ok, there have been some improvements to the cover, but I believe the really significant ones have happened on the inside.

The analogy should be clear. While we can make changes for the better to our bodies, more time should be spent improving our inside, that is our minds, hearts and souls. For sure, we should take care of our bodies. It's the only one we have and it is our temple. However, the changes that make us useful to God are made in our hearts. This starts with having Christ in the center of our lives. The Bible tells us that we are all vessels, some for honor, and some for dishonor. In other words, some vessels are used to drink from and others we put garbage in. We should strive to be a vessel of honor for God. By searching for His guidance through prayer and study, the Holy Spirit can begin to polish your heart for great things. He will transform you from the inside out. Be patient because it takes time for a craftsman to polish a precious metal to a high finish. You will be amazed at the results.

SWING THOUGHT FOR THE DAY

On the other hand, discipline yourself for the purpose of godliness; for bodily discipline is only of little profit, but godliness is profitable for all things, since it holds promise for the present life and also for the life to come. It is a trustworthy statement deserving full acceptance. For it is for this we labor and strive, because we have fixed our hope on the living God, who is the Savior of all men, especially of believers. Prescribe and teach these things. **I Timothy 4: 7b-10**

Day 14

MAINTAIN YOUR COMPOSURE

How do you react when, after going through your preshot routine and making your practice swing, you execute an unbelievably poor shot. Maybe it goes in the water or stays in the bunker. You know what I mean. You want to throw a club or perhaps let a few curse words fly. Remember, golf is a gentleman's game. Maintaining your composure will impress your friends and help on the next shot. I've seen some great players chunk shots in the water, shank balls dead right, 3 putt, 4 putt and yes, even 5 putt. Yet almost all of them hold their composure. Just by looking at them you would never know anything bad had just happened. How do they do that? Well, it takes a lot of discipline. Your mind must stay in charge of your emotions. Only then can you make your body perform consistently. Behaving like this on the golf course will gain you a good reputation and others will want to be around you. This is part of being a mature person.

Our Christian walk should mirror this as well. Many times in the New Testament, Paul encourages us to buffet or discipline our bodies and make them behave. We should live our lives in such a way that we are noticeably different at work, school or play. Our behavior should be marked with a quiet confidence. We should be slow to cry foul and even slower to retaliate when wronged. If we live our lives just as the world does, our faith is not very strong. We must remember that a large portion of our witness is how we live out our faith. A lack of composure on our part could cause one to stumble. Truly, we may be the only Jesus some will ever see. Therefore, we must learn to take the peaks and valleys that life and the golf course, for that matter, gives us with style and grace. When we can do this, we can become all that God wants us to be. So, no matter what happens, hold your finish. You won't be sorry.

SWING THOUGHT FOR THE DAY

Do you not know that those who run in a race all run, but only one receives the prize?
Run in such a way that you may win. Therefore I run in such a way, as not without
aim; I box in such a way, as not beating the air: But I buffet my body, and make
it my slave, lest possibly after I have preached to others, I myself should
be disqualified. ***I Corinthians 9: 24, 26-27***

Day 15

THE RIGHT POSTURE

Like many of you, I have my usual foursome. We play our home course on most Saturdays, weather permitting. It was on one of these occasions that God used an errant shot to teach an important lesson. On the back nine, the first par three is hole number twelve. Like most par threes there is a premium placed on hitting the ball straight. From the white tees its 160 yards to the center of a very shallow green which is then guarded on the front by a deep bunker. There is a little bale out room on the right but too far right and you are in serious trouble. On this particular Saturday, I blocked my shot and sailed into the woods far right of the green. I searched for my ball but was unsuccessful. I was ready to give up and take my medicine, stroke and distance, when my playing partner began pointing from several yards away. He kept pointing but I could not see the ball. Finally, I got down on my knees and there it was. I could now see my ball.

It was there that God taught me that sometimes you can only see what you are looking for from your knees. It is there in those quiet moments, just you and God, that you can improve your spiritual eye sight and begin to see things and people as God sees them. This was a big moment for me. The next time you are searching for the tough answers to life's questions and problems, try seeking those answers from your knees in prayer. God is a great listener and gives perfect advice. Oh yeah, as far as that par three went, I was able to punch the ball out, chip and one putt for a bogey.

SWING THOUGHT FOR THE DAY

Thus says the LORD, the Holy One of Israel, and his Maker: Ask me about the things to come concerning my sons, and you shall commit to Me the work of My hands. It is I who made the earth, and created man upon it. I stretched out the heavens with my hands,
and I ordained all their host. Turn to me, and be saved, all the ends of the
earth: for I am God, and there is no other. I have sworn by Myself, the
word is gone forth from my mouth in righteousness, and will not turn
back, that to Me every knee shall bow, every tongue will swear allegiance. **Isaiah 45: 11-12, 22-23**

Day 16

TAKE A MULLIGAN

Every group or foursome has a set of local rules. My foursome has them and so does yours. One of ours is a mulligan off of the first tee, one do over, a second chance. Golf is a second chance game. Many times I have had a lousy front nine and have managed to right myself and play well on the back nine resulting in a pretty good score. On other occasions, I have hit a terrible tee shot, executed a good recovery shot, chipped up and one putted for par. Golf is like that and I think God is too. I believe God is a second chance God. He refreshes our spirit each day. He initiates His love toward us over and over. Do you remember the woman in John, Chapter 8? She was caught in the act of adultery. During Jesus' day, this was a sin worthy of death. After the Pharisees had their say, what did Jesus do? Did He quote the rules and regulations of the day? No, He forgave her, told her to go her way and sin no more. Now that is refreshing. Once in a while, a really poor shot will hit a tree or cart path and end up in the middle of the fairway. When that happens, take advantage of it. When God gives you a second chance, do the same.

Just as the perfect round of golf will never be played, except for Jesus, the perfect life will never be lived. There will be days where things go wrong, episodes in your life that you will wish you could undo and words spoken in anger that you wish you could take back. Unfortunately, you cannot. Remember though, God is there, waiting to listen and forgive. Further, He is faithful to help you improve and right any wrong. Finally, what matters most is not what you did, but what you will do next. Go on, take a mulligan.

Swing Thought for the Day

"Now in the Law Moses commanded us to stone such women;
what then do you say?" But when they persisted in asking Him,
He straightened up, and said to them, "He who is without sin
among you, let him be the first to throw a stone at her." And
again He stooped down,
and wrote on the ground. And when they heard it, they began to
go out one by one,
beginning with the older ones, and He was left alone, and the
woman, where
she had been, in the midst. And straightening up, Jesus said to
her,
"Woman, where are they? Did no one condemn you?" And
she said, "No one, Lord." And Jesus said, "Neither
do I condemn you, go your way and from now
on sin no more." **John 8: 5,7-11**

Day 17

PLAYING PARTNERS

As we go through life, we tend accumulate stuff. If you ask most people about this, they will tell you about all the things they have collected over the years. I want to mention some that maybe you have not thought about. Two such things are relationships and accomplishments. Have you ever thought about which is more important, relationships or accomplishments? In my opinion, it is definitely relationships. Let me explain. Occasionally, I enjoy playing golf by myself. I enjoy being outdoors and appreciate the beauty of the course and God's handy work. However, when I come to the par 3's, I am always a little apprehensive. Why? Well, for one thing, I have never had a hole in one. And if I happen to hit that perfect shot and the ball goes into the hole. If no one sees it, it may not count. You need a witness or relationship for the really big things in life to be meaningful and to be able to enjoy them to the fullest. So you see, accomplishments without relationships do not count for much.

Stop for a minute and think about those relationships you have in your life. Think about those you love. Several times in the New Testament, Jesus encouraged us to love God first and foremost. Secondly, He said for us to love each other. Are you doing that? Do you tell those close to you that you love them? Take the time to develop and nourish good relationships. These will be the things in life that will last and provide you with the most return on your investment. Make sure, too, that your relationship with Jesus is what it should be. Without Christ in your life, all the accomplishments of a life time will still leave you feeling empty. Jesus wants a personal relationship with you. Let Him play along with you on your next round. Give Him the honors.

SWING THOUGHT FOR THE DAY

Do nothing from selfishness or empty conceit, but with humility
of mind let each of you regard
one another as more important than himself; do not merely look
out for your own
personal interests, but also for the interests of others.
Philippians 2:3-4

Day 18

ONE SHOT AT A TIME

Do you ever listen to the interviews of golfers after a successful round? If you do, you have probably heard phrases like these, "I tried to be patient out there today", "I took what the golf course gave me", "I played within myself" or "I just had to grind it out for par". What does all this mean? I think I can sum it up this way. Successful golfers have the ability to stay in the moment and play one shot at a time. They are able to concentrate on executing the next shot and forgetting everything else. They don't worry about making a 4 foot putt when they are 150 yards away from the green. Moreover, they are able to focus on the target and the target only. You see, on the golf course there are various hazards that need to be successfully negotiated and avoided. Hazards, such as water or bunkers come into play when your eye leaves the target and begins to focus them. Now, for sure, you don't ignore these potential problems. You prepare for them, account for them and play accordingly based on your skill.

God wants us to approach life in the same way. That is, one day at a time. For sure, He wants us to prepare for the future. But He also wants us to enjoy the present. Obviously, we should have retirement accounts, car insurance and termite protection for our homes. But these should not consume us and occupy all of our time and money. Do you remember when Peter saw our Lord coming to the disciples on the water? Peter asked if he could get out of the boat and walk on the water to Jesus. Peter did fine as long as he kept his eyes on Jesus. However, he began to sink when he took his eyes off of Him and began to look at how rough the sea was. So, whether in golf or life, your chances of success are greatly improved if you keep you eye on the target, not the problems that come along. I am reminded of what Harvey Penick said, "Take dead aim". Do this and watch your scores improve.

SWING THOUGHT FOR THE DAY

But seek first His kingdom and His righteousness; and all these things shall be added
to you. Therefore do not be anxious for tomorrow; for tomorrow will care for itself.
Each day has enough trouble of its own. ***Matthew 6: 33-34***

Day 19

THE SCORE CARD

Each time you play a round of golf, you enter your score on the score card. Each golf course has its own score card. Information on the card will give you a clue as to the difficulty of the course. These include the course rating, the slope, the yardages from the different tees and the score necessary for par. Knowing these before your round will help you make decisions that will make the round more enjoyable. And, while you may be competing against a friend or playing in a tournament, ultimately, you are competing against the golf course itself. Great players of the game will tell you they really don't worry about what their competitors are doing until there are just a few holes left. Generally, they will concentrate on the golf course and how to position themselves to achieve the best score. Winners understand how they are measured and what they are measured against.

Many aspects of our Christian walk are like this as well. Just as some golf courses are more difficult than others, some days, weeks or even years will be tougher than others. One class in school will give us trouble. A professor will be unreasonable. Our job may not satisfy us. We may not get along with a coworker or superior. Remember that we should do all we do as though it is for our Lord. This will help you protect your Christian witness. Remember too, that God does not measure us against each other. It's easy to compare ourselves to others and make ourselves look good. Too often we dismiss our own shortcomings by unfair comparisons. This allows sin, though small, to live in our hearts and perhaps go unchecked. The yardstick we should be using is the One God sent, that is Jesus. To improve our spiritual life, use Jesus as your measure, on the course use par. You'll win more competitions this way.

SWING THOUGHT FOR THE DAY

And whatever you do in word or deed, do all in the name of the Lord Jesus, giving
thanks through Him to God the Father. Whatever you do, do your work heartily,
as for the Lord rather than for men; knowing that from the Lord you will
receive the reward of the inheritance. It is the Lord Christ whom you serve. **Colossians 3: 17, 23**

Day 20

LOWER YOUR HANDICAP

Do you know what your handicap is? Do you know what a handicap is? Well, it is a calculation involving the best 10 scores of your last 20 rounds. The calculation is made using the following equation:

(10 Best Rounds Differential/10) x .96
(The slope & rating of the courses you played may also be involved.)

It gives you a numerical indication of how close you are to being a scratch golfer or scoring par. It is also gives you an indication if you are getting better or worse, depending on whether it is going down or up, (the lower, the better). Generally speaking, as you become a more proficient golfer, your scores come down and so does your handicap. Usually this happens incrementally. Rarely, do people improve dramatically after just a few rounds. Few golfers begin to play and then cut their handicap several points at a time. To lower your handicap, it takes practice and sometimes personal instruction. Your handicap cannot be lowered just by playing round after round. You need a plan, for me it was private lessons. Also, I have a tune up lesson every spring. After 6 years, I have successfully cut my handicap in half.

In life, we should strive to improve by becoming more and more like Christ. Becoming more like Christ will involve making changes to your life, probably a lot of them. These changes, like the ones to improve your golf game, should be systematic and fairly small. Those who make giant leaps in Christ likeness, especially when it happens in a short amount of time, generally don't last. Like lowering your handicap, becoming more like Christ happens a little at a time. Seek to find things each day that will change your life. Spend time alone with God. Spend time with other Christians in worship. Study the Word. Pray often. Then, little by little, you will begin to take on the likeness of our Lord. From now on, when you think about your handicap, think about your Christ likeness too.

SWING THOUGHT FOR THE DAY

Therefore be imitators of God, as beloved children; and walk in love, just as Christ also loved you, and gave Himself up for us, and offering and a sacrifice to God as a fragrant aroma. Walk as children of light for the fruit of the light consists in all goodness and righteousness and truth, trying to learn what is pleasing to the Lord. **Ephesians 5: 1-2, 8b-10**

Day 21

REJOICE

Have you ever noticed that in almost every town, church or even golf course, there are a few people who don't want to see anything good happen to others? They seem to enjoy and relish in the misery of their fellow man. I have always wondered why this is the case. For me, it is particularly disturbing when this attitude extends itself to the golf course. I have seen golfers root against their competitors, hoping they will mis-hit a shot or pull a putt left. Statistics show that there is danger in doing this. Data on this subject show that golfers who practice this attitude usually play worse themselves. You see they are using up a certain amount of their ability to concentrate on things that are out of their control, rather than attending to their own game. Tour players will tell you that they expect their fellow players to hit every green and make every putt. In doing so, they stay in the moment and stay focused on what they can control. Practicing this attitude will result in lower scores. This will hold true whether you are on tour or just playing your Saturday foursome.

The Apostle Paul encourages us, Roman 12, to rejoice with those who rejoice and weep with those who weep. In other words, we should be happy when good things happen to those around us. Too often this is not the case. Many people seem to enjoy seeing others struggle or do poorly. Learn to be glad when others do well on or off the golf course. If someone at work gets promoted, congratulate them. If someone at school does well on an exam, praise them. If your competitor sinks a 40 foot putt, shake his hand. I think you get the idea. Developing this trait will make you someone that others want to be with and you will soon find that your attitude and personality will be more Christ like. I believe this would have made Paul happy. I'm sure he would rejoice.

SWING THOUGHT FOR THE DAY

Rejoice in the Lord always; again I will say, rejoice! Let your forbearing spirit be known to
all men. The Lord is near. Be anxious for nothing, but in everything by prayer and
supplication with thanksgiving let your requests be made known to God. And
the peace of God, which surpasses all comprehension, shall guard your
hearts and your minds in Christ Jesus. ***Philippians 4: 4-7***

Day 22

YARDAGE MARKERS

On most golf courses, markers have been placed to let you know how far, or near for that matter, you are from the center of the green. Many times there are markers at 200 yards, usually blue, at 150 yards, sometimes a white stake, and at 100 yards, often a red marker. Better courses have yardages marked off on the sprinkler heads. Knowing these distances are critical to a successful approach shot. Without them, you would have to count on your own sense of depth perception and distance. These little markers may seem insignificant at the time. However, they, both individually and collectively, play an important role in posting a low quality score. They are put there by the ones who built and run the golf course. They are there to help us play better golf. Most players look for these markers and trust them.

During every round of golf, you will pass several dozen yardage markers. Also, during your walk on this Earth, you will be provided with markers as well. These markers or touch stones will help ground you. They will be different for everyone. Yet they will, overtime, help define who we are and will teach us about God and His goodness. Some will be pleasant and uplifting, while others will cause us great pain. Markers in our lives may be graduation, marriage or the birth of a child. Others may be the death of a parent, a divorce or a catastrophic illness. Just as in golf, these markers are put there by the One who made us. They let us know of His presence. They tell us we are getting closer to our heavenly home. Wise men still look for these, embrace them and grow from them. Knowing where we are on or off the golf course is critical to our success. So check your yardage. Are you closer to God today than you were yesterday? Walk closer with God today.

SWING THOUGHT FOR THE DAY

Therefore thus says the LORD God, "Behold, I am laying in Zion a stone, a tested stone, a costly cornerstone for the foundation, firmly placed. He who believes in it will not be disturbed." **Isaiah 28: 16**

Day 23

BOUNDARIES

You have heard it said that golf is a much easier game when played from the short grass. We all know this to be true. However, from time to time, you will find yourself far from the fairway. And, on occasion, you may even find yourself in a water hazard, a lateral hazard or even out of bounds. According to the rules, these are marked with a red, yellow and white stakes, respectively. Even the tee box has markers that you must be between before teeing off. When your ball lands in one of these hazards or ends up out of bounds, the rules allow you to recover. But, there are inevitable consequences. These usually range from a one or two stroke penalty up to stroke and distance. The point here is there are consequences to hitting a ball outside the normal playing area or boundaries of the golf course. Doing this makes a good score much more difficult and increases your frustration.

Similar to golf, life comes with boundaries. I believe God made these boundaries, not to keep us from having fun, but He put them in place for our protection. If you think about it, we have boundaries all around us. The double yellow line on the highway separates us from oncoming traffic. Civil and criminal laws protect us from those who would do us harm. The Bible tells us that God does not withhold any good thing from us. However, with these freedoms comes a set of boundaries to keep us from getting hurt. Staying within these God-set boundaries keeps our hearts clean from sin and often protects our physical health too. For instance, God gave us the gift of sex. But, He set up the boundary of marriage. If we go outside of God's boundaries, we forfeit His built in protection. The consequences of this type of sin can be severe physically, spiritually and emotionally. So, to maintain your Christian walk, stay inside of the limits that God has set. On the golf course, keep it in the short grass.

SWING THOUGHT FOR THE DAY

I have called you by name; you are mine! When you pass through the waters,
I will be with you; and through the rivers, they will not overflow you,
when you walk through the fire, you will not be scorched, nor will
the flame burn you. For I am the LORD your God, the Holy One of Israel, your Savior. ***Isaiah 43: 1b-3a***

Day 24

PATIENCE

Have you ever tried to get a round of golf in when you really didn't have time? I have and truthfully it was no fun. Golf is a sport that forces you to be patient. It requires you to take your time in order to make good decisions on club selection, course management and reading of the greens. For some, this can be difficult because we have been conditioned by ATMs, microwave ovens and drive through windows that tell us faster is better. Now don't get me wrong, I don't enjoy six hour rounds of golf. However, part of the enjoyment of a round of golf should be experiencing your surroundings, especially on courses you play for the first time. Take time to appreciate the landscaping, the wildlife indigenous to the area and the architectural beauty of the golf course itself. If you have time, walk the course. Do this and I'll bet you will relax and play better golf. Patience is perhaps the one attribute of an accomplished golfer that can't be faked.

So how does being patient or developing patience apply to our Christian walk? Well, if we are not careful, we will tend to hurry through our lives without actually taking time to enjoy it. We spend too much of our lives rushing here and there, and before you know it, a good portion of your time here on Earth has evaporated. The point here is simple. God made a wonderful place for us live with an endless variety of things to excite our five senses. Take time to enjoy them. He also gave us friends and loved ones to develop lasting relationships to share in these experiences. Finally, I believe Christ, while here on Earth, was very patient. We should be like Him in this way too. Patience is not something we are born with, it must be developed by act of the will. Exercising patience on the golf course will lead to better decisions and lower scores. Exercising patience in your every day life will lead to a full and satisfying life. Patience is a virtue that too few have and even fewer use regularly. Learning patience and being patient with those around us is a great way to demonstrate God's love. It shows that we have indeed overcome the world. Use is liberally, beginning today.

SWING THOUGHT FOR THE DAY

Be patient, therefore, brethren, until the coming of the Lord.
Behold, the farmer waits
for the precious produce of the soil, being patient about it, until
it gets the early
and late rains. You too be patient; strengthen your hearts, for the
coming of the Lord is at hand. ***James 5: 7-8***

Day 25

COURSE MANAGEMENT

During every round of golf, you will make many choices. Do you go for the green in two or lay up? Do you hit a strong 9 iron or a smooth 8? Can you carry the fairway bunker off of the tee or do you play away from it? Is the putt straight or does it break to the left? As you can see you will make hundreds of decisions or choices while playing golf. And with every choice made, there is a result or consequence. With every decision you make on the course, you will enjoy the result or suffer the consequence. Ultimately, the choices we make will determine the outcome of our efforts and affect our score. The trick then, is to make consistently good decisions and properly manage the golf course. You have to know when to go for it and when to play it safe. You have to lean on your strengths and confront your weaknesses. You have to be honest with yourself with respect to your limitations. When you make good decisions on a consistent basis, your scores will, more often than not, be better.

By now you know that golf mirrors life in several ways and this is another one. Hazards, bunkers and bad lies are not only found on golf courses, they are also found in life too. Not always, but in many cases we land in these due to a choice we made. Everyday, we are confronted with a myriad of decisions and choices to make. Often, little thought is given to these potentially life changing choices. The Bible is full of examples of both good and poor decisions. These are accompanied by their respective results, sometimes victories, at other times disasters. Again, the trick is to live our lives where we are consistently making good decisions. The ability to make good decisions, whether in life or on the golf course, is no accident. This ability is the result of spending time with the One who knows you best. Do you remember those simple bracelets with the letters, "WWJD" on them? They stand for, 'What would Jesus do?" If you are not sure about something you are about to do, it is still a good question to ask.

SWING THOUGHT FOR THE DAY

A wise man will hear and increase in learning, and a man of understanding will acquire wise counsel, to understand a proverb and a figure, the words of the wise and their riddles. The fear of the LORD is the beginning of knowledge; fools despise wisdom and instruction. **Proverbs 1: 5-7**

Day 26

IT'S SIMPLE, WASH AND BE CLEAN

In the spring of 2005, I shot the round of my life, a 73. That's right, a one over par 73. I actually had a birdie putt on 18 for an even par 72 and missed it. Later in the week, after I had told practically everyone I knew about it, I had a chance to reflect on that wonderful spring Saturday afternoon. As I thought about it, God used it to teach me another lesson in life. You see, for those four hours, golf was a simple thing to me. I was not concerned about the mechanics of the golf swing, whether my stance was open or closed, if the club face was square to the target, or if the wind was into me or with me. Golf was simple, take the club back, drop it down on the ball and watch it go. I tell you it was a magical day. For those of you that play golf, you know what I mean. There is no other feeling like it.

Now, what has this got to do with our Christian walk? Well, I was reminded of the Old Testament story about a man named Naaman found in 2nd Kings. He was a great warrior and captain of the Syrian army, a mighty man of valor. Along with all of these things, he was also a leper. This kept him isolated from his countrymen and prevented him from participating in many of the activities in which he would have otherwise have been invited. Naaman was told by a slave girl that he could be healed if he went to see the prophet Elisha. He imagined that he would be asked to do some great thing and that in return Elisha would come out, have this huge ceremonial cleansing and Naaman would be healed. Well, it didn't happen that way. In fact, Elisha did not even come out of his house. He simply sent word telling Naaman to go to the Jordon River and dip seven times. Basically, he told him to "Wash and be clean". Naaman couldn't believe it was so simple, but eventually followed the command and was made whole. I think God was using this event to get us ready for Jesus' coming. Jesus, too, gives us a simple command to wash and be clean. Over the centuries, men have tried to complicate this process by adding other requirements that are not found in the Bible. It's still as simple as it was for Naaman. Is there sin in your life? If so, it's simple, wash and be clean.

SWING THOUGHT FOR THE DAY

Then his servants came near, and spoke to him and said, "My father, if the prophet
had told you to do some great thing, would you not have done it? How much
rather then, when he says to you, Wash, and be clean?" **II Kings**
5: 13

Day 27

KEEP IT SIMPLE

Several years ago, after a successful business meeting, I took a customer to the local golf course for a friendly round. Being an engineer, he was very good at his work. He was very analytical in his approach to running the business. On the golf course, however, this proved to be his undoing. And on that day, mine as well. After every swing, he would inundate me with what seemed to be dozens of questions about his swing. Was his head still, did he transfer his weight, did he cock his left wrist, was his hip turn done properly and on and on. You get the idea. After about four holes of this, my game was completely shot. To be a consistent golfer, you cannot clutter your mind with an endless number of swing thoughts. If you talk with really accomplished golfers, they will tell you that during each practice session or round, they only have a few swing thoughts. They then, will concentrate on these and these only. The thoughts may change from week to week, but each time they will only have a few. I just don't think your mind can handle too many inputs.

Like wise, if we are listening, I believe God gives us a few spiritual concepts and Bible verses each week for us to dwell on to help us become a more consistent Christian. This approach allows us to meditate on a finite amount of information and really soak it into our minds, hearts, and souls. This gives us a steady flow of new truths, displacing thoughts that are perhaps not very pleasing to our Lord. Learn to do this and you will not only improve your golf swing but you will improve your Christian lifestyle as well.

SWING THOUGHT FOR THE DAY

So He said, "go forth, and stand on the mountain before the LORD." And, behold, the
LORD was passing by, and a great and strong wind was rending the mountains,
and breaking in pieces the rocks before the LORD; but the LORD was not in
the wind. And after the wind an earthquake; but the LORD was not in the
earthquake. And after the earthquake a fire; but the LORD was not
in the fire; and after the fire a still small voice.
I Kings 19: 11-12

Day 28

IT'S YOUR HONOR

Terms like honor, honesty and integrity over that last several years have had their meanings transformed. The meanings used to be objective. However, lately they have become subjective terms where it all depends. It is refreshing to see that the true meaning of these words is still alive and well on the golf course. I am amazed to see how pro golfers behave when it comes to maintaining the integrity of the game. You see, golf is a sport where most penalties are not called by a third party such as a referee or umpire. Most penalties are called by the golfers and most of those are called by the golfer on himself. Let me give you an example. During the 2004 British Open, there was a golfer who was getting ready to putt out when his ball moved. The wind was blowing hard and caused the ball to roll ever so slightly. Because he had addressed the ball, that constituted a one stroke penalty and he had to put the ball back where it was. The unusual thing here is that no one saw this happen but the golfer himself. He could have just let it go. After all, no one would know. And, it could cost him thousands of dollars or it could make him miss the cut. What did he do? What would you do? Well, he called the penalty and added a stroke to his score on that hole. By today's standards that is rare.

You know, I would like to think that we would all do the same. However, think about how we deal with sin in our lives. If you are like me, most of the sins I commit, no one knows about. We can sin and more often than not, it goes unnoticed by our peers. What should we do about that? We could check to make sure no one saw us and then just forget it. I think that God wants us to do what that golfer did. We should call the penalty on ourselves and ask for forgiveness. Most of the time, we can do this privately, just God and you. Sometimes you may need to go to others and ask for their forgiveness. That would be like adding a stroke to your score. God is faithful to forgive. By making such calls on themselves, pro golfers protect the integrity of the game. And, when we confess our sins before God, we protect the integrity of our love for Him. Honor the game, honor Him.

SWING THOUGHT FOR THE DAY

Be gracious to me, O God, according to thy loving-kindness: according to the greatness of thy compassion blot out my transgressions. Wash me thoroughly from my iniquity, and cleanse
me from my sin. Wash me and I shall be whiter than snow.
Psalms 51: 1-2, 7b

Day 29

CONFIDENCE

Confidence on the golf course is an elusive and sometimes fleeting thing. A golf club may be the only implement that can show both total confidence and the complete absence of it. Golf balls struck with confidence rise form the club face in an almost majestic way with a boring flight to the target. The same player, when he is unsure and allows doubt to creep in, can strike the same ball with the same club and it will go weakly to the right. Why is this so? There are many reasons but I think the main one is that a lack of confidence is a product of what is going on in the player's mind and heart as the decision is made on how to hit the next shot. We have all seen professional golfers strike balls with total confidence for the first 3 rounds of a tournament. Then, in an almost unexplainable way, their confidence departs, leaving them to collapse on Sunday afternoon. Most of the time, they never know what happened or why. If you have a passion for golf, it is one of the saddest events you can witness.

As Christians, we will all go through the highs and lows of life. This includes going through times of great confidence and a lack of it resulting in despair. Christians are not immune to these swings regardless of whether you have a golf club in your hand or not. However, I believe you can minimize the effects. I have found at least three ways that seem to help me regain my confidence. First, I have found that humming a favorite hymn helps me to clear my mind. Second, I think about a favorite scripture. This reminds me of how much God loves me. Finally, the most effective way that I have found to re-instill confidence in my game and life is to take a couple of minutes to dwell on those in my life who love me with an unconditional love. You know, your loved ones who accept you just the way you are. When I do this, my confidence often returns and I save my round, or at least the rest of my day. Find your 3 things and use them like swing thoughts. I bet they will help.

SWING THOUGHT FOR THE DAY

Yet those who wait for the LORD will gain new strength; they will mount up with
wings like eagles, they will run and not get tired, they will walk and not become
weary. "Do not fear, for I am with you; Do not anxiously look about you,
for I am our God. I will strengthen you, surely I will help you, surely I
will uphold you with My righteous right hand."
Isaiah 40:31, 41:10

Day 30

THE CADDIE

How important do you think a good caddie is on tour? They never take a single shot for the player, but few pros could win on tour without a competent caddie. Caddies perform all sorts of tasks to assure the success of their pro. Before each tournament, they check to assure the player has the right clubs for the course and the right number of clubs in the bag. He walks the course to check yardages and makes notes of obstacles and hazards that should be avoided as well as landing areas that would assure acceptable approach shots. During the tournament, caddies will assist in the warm up routines and make sure his player is on time. He will help read the greens and keep his player focused. Maybe the most important thing caddies do is instill confidence in their player. Further, the caddie is the player's biggest cheerleader, making sure there is no doubt in the player's mind that the shot he is about to make is the right one. This sort of camaraderie and teamwork is seldom seen in sports. Properly handled, this relationship can make for great success on the golf course.

God made us to be social creatures. God said early on that it is not good for us to be alone. And, while it is possible to worship our Lord in solitude, I believe the experience is more meaningful if we worship together.

So what do a caddie and a tour player have in common with our Christian walk? Well, one way that we, as Christians, can help each other is to be accountability partners. Accountability partners meet an important need in our lives. They help keep us grounded. He or she, (I have found that accountability partners work better if they are of the same sex.) is someone who will listen without judgment and someone you can confess your sins to without condemnation. In short, this person is someone who you can share your heart with and who will support you in your efforts. At the same time, they will hold you accountable when you begin to miss the mark. If you don't have an accountability partner, pray about this and seek them out today.

SWING THOUGHT FOR THE DAY

Give instruction to a wise man, and he will be still wiser, teach a righteous man, and he will increase his learning. The fear of the LORD is the beginning of wisdom, and the knowledge of the Holy One is understanding. The way of a fool is right in his own eyes.
But a wise man is he who listens to counsel.
Proverbs 9:9-10, 12:15

Day 31

SAVING PAR

Finally, I want to leave you with one last example. Only this time, it is an example from the golf course that does not reflect God's truth or His nature. When you stand on the tee box of a typical par 4 there are many options to make par that can and should be considered. Many thoughts will go through your mind. You could hit your driver or play it safe with a fairway wood. Next, you could hit a full 7 iron or maybe a knockdown 5 iron to keep it under the wind. Around the green you may choose to hit a flop shot with a lob wedge or bump and run with a 9 iron. Finally, you could putt it in by dying it to the hole or take the break out of it by firming it to the back of the cup. In short, there are all sorts of ways to get the ball in the cup. You may reach your goal of par using one of several routes that have just been described. No matter which way you choose, a 4 is written on the score card.

However, to reach the goal of eternal life, there is only one way. That way is Jesus Christ. Jesus made it clear that no one comes to the Father except through Him. The Apostle Paul warned us not to compete only to be disqualified. In the rules of golf, there are a few infractions that will disqualify you from the competition. Serious players rarely break them. The lesson should be clear. Don't live your life in such a way that you will be disqualified from eternal life with Him. Accept Jesus as you Savior today. Ask Him to live in your heart. Be sure of your salvation. Enjoy your life by walking with God daily. Enjoy the greatest game ever created.

SWING THOUGHT FOR THE DAY

Let not your heart be troubled; believe in God, believe also in Me. In My Father's house
are many dwelling places; if it were not so, I would have told you; for I go to prepare
a place for you. And if I go and prepare a place for you, I will come again, and
receive you to Myself; that where I am, there you may be also. I am the way,
and the truth, and the life; no one comes to the Father, but through me. ***John 14: 1-3, 6***

Breinigsville, PA USA
05 February 2010
231959BV00001B/1/P